MW00876060

Dallas Willard

Called to Business
God's way of loving people through business and the professions

DALLAS WILLARD
MINISTRIES
Living in the kingdom now

ISBN: 978-1-7901-3003-0
ISBN-13: 978-1-7901-3003-0-13

Library of Congress Cataloging-in-Publication Data
Willard, Dallas, 1935-2013, author.
Called to Business: God's way of loving people through business and
    the professions / Dallas Willard. — First edition.

Images: Cover photo by Denys Nevozhai

Printed in the United States of America

Table of Contents

Introduction
By Dallas Willard (2001)[1]

Human beings are situated in a world structured by small and large systems of hidden powers. On the physical side, the wheel and the lever, heat (fire, steam, internal combustion engines), electricity, and the atom are all illustrations of the unfolding destiny of humanity upon the earth. That destiny is, in biblical language, "to have dominion" (Genesis 1:26). That is, we are to be responsible for the earth and life upon it. Human inventions or discoveries are all related, in straightforward ways, to work. Work is the production of value by the actions of our thoughts and bodily efforts upon available resources.

What's more, work is a good thing, and it is a natural disposition of human beings from early childhood on. Work is simply human creativity. It is a special type of causation through which goodness and blessing can be promoted in our surroundings.

---

[1] First published as the Foreword in Bill Heatley, *The Gift of Work*, NavPress, 2008.

1

Except in the rare "desert island" kinds of cases, the values produced by work, and the particular activities involved in work, are social or communal in nature. They are strictly inconceivable except in a communal setting, from the family on up. They depend upon others for their existence, and they are for the benefit of others as well as of the individual worker. This too is "a good thing" and part of God's arrangement for the virtue and prospering of human beings. Without a "division of labor" and suitable human relationships in community, human life can barely rise above the level of animals. So the great question is: What is the "resource" that will enable human beings, developing the powers of nature, to live in a community where there is dignity, love, and provision for everyone?

We know very well some of the human answers to this vital question, and we have the bitter experience of their failures. The modern answers all focus upon the matter of "ownership." That is, upon the question of who shall have the right to say what will be done with the "resources." One says that the state or government should own the means (including money and human labor) by which goods are produced. That is Socialism. (But the "state" turns out in practice just to be certain people, who may be neither wise nor competent nor good.) Communism says that no one should own those means of production. (But then it turns out that certain people do, for all practical purposes—regardless of the "official" arrangement.) Unrestrained Capitalism says that enterprising individuals should own them, catch as catch can in "fair" competition. (But then "*fair*" gets defined by those who have the goods.)

None of these "answers," we should now know, provides a moral solution to the human problems posed by work. In simple terms, this is because none of them deal with the fine texture of human motivation: with what men and women care about and live for. They are a form of the proverbial "brain surgery with a meat cleaver." The popular theories of human action now taught in our best schools of "management" do little better.

We must address the fundamental problem of finding appropriate community-in-work for human beings. That community is the resource without which all other resources languish or become dangerous. Finding this community must be addressed at the level where work is done in a world not really structured around doing what is good and right, but around doing it my way and for my benefit. That is the level of the job. (Spelled, incidentally, just like the name of the all-time leader in suffering, Job. What a coincidence!) The only meaningful solution is that of Jesus Christ and His followers. It is the recognition of, and intelligent reliance upon, the community (Kingdom, Family) of God. That community is already there at your job, waiting to turn it back into rich and rewarding and meaningful work, creativity, shared production of goods to be shared. You don't make God's community, of course—you receive it, by counting on it and acting with it.

The accessibility of life in the community of God to every person was the message of Jesus, in His words and in His deeds. Everything else fits into that: forgiveness of sins, redemption from sin, transformation of character into "righteousness, peace, and joy in the Holy Spirit" (Romans 14:17), transformation of society, and the development of history into everlasting life. In His efforts to help those around Him understand the message and reality of the community of God, Jesus on one occasion remarked that the community of God is not recognized by eyesight. It isn't something localizable in the world, like a human social group, a government (buildings), or an army. Rather, He said, it is already there, "in your midst" (Luke 17:21). That is to say, it is already where you are, wherever that may be, right now.

Now that was not a new thing in the time of Jesus, though it was for Him alone to manifest and to be its full meaning. In Deuteronomy, we read that God's word, and doing what He wants and supports, "is not too difficult for you, nor is it out of reach. It is not in heaven, that you should say, 'Who will go up to heaven for us to get it for us and make us hear it, that we may observe [do] it?' Nor is it beyond the sea... . But the word is very near you, in your mouth and in your heart, that you may observe [do] it" (30:11-14). The twenty-third psalm is a poetic celebration of this life in "the Everlasting Arms" (Deuteronomy 33:27).

Paul, taught by Christ Himself, reclaims and enlarges this vision of our life in God (Romans 10:8). He tells his Philippian friends: "Our citizenship" (πολίτευμα)—our "socio-economic" order, if you wish, or our "commonwealth"—is in the heavens (3:20). That means it is right around us ("in our midst"), not something far away and at

4

some later time. We are *now*, as disciples of Jesus, members of a divine community that, when we seek it, we find with us in our job and throughout life: and thereby we turn all that we do into work for and under God. Thus, Paul advises: "Whatever you do, do your work heartily—literally, 'from the soul'—as for the Lord rather than for men, knowing that from the Lord you will receive the reward of the inheritance. It is the Lord Christ whom you serve" (Colossians 3:23-24). We are not to try to look good (do "eye service"), as men-pleasers, but on our job we simply "do the will of God from the soul" (Ephesians 6:6-8).

So how do we apply this Kingdom community truth in the real-life context of the job: on what really goes on there, and how, for our part, we can turn it into divine work? It requires a life that is spiritual throughout, full of meaning, strength, and joy. We must seek to find a way to stand in the solid tradition of Christian teaching throughout the ages. We must do so with the freshness of personal experience and with the forcefulness of careful thought.

Phillips Brooks was a great American pastor and teacher of a century ago. He was for a long time the pastor of one of the greatest churches in the United States, and sometimes the Anglican Bishop of Massachusetts; but he was also a man of national prominence and influence. In his sermon, "Best Methods of Promoting Spiritual Life," he acknowledges the role of special religious practices, activities, and experiences. But he goes on to emphasize that to limit spirituality to these is to omit most of our life from spiritual living. To

5

promote spiritual life, he says, is not to be more religious where one is already religious:

> It is to be religious where he is irreligious now; to let the spiritual force which is in him play upon new activities. How shall he open, for instance, his business life to this deep power? By casting out of his business all that is essentially wicked in it, by insisting to himself on its ideal, of charity or usefulness, on the loftiest conception of every relationship into which it brings him with his fellow man, and by making it not a matter of his own whim or choice, but a duty to be done faithfully because God has called him to it... God chose for him his work, and meant for him to find his spiritual education there.[2]

Brooks closed his sermon with these words: "The Christian finds the hand of Christ in everything, and by the faithful use of everything for Christ's sake, he takes firm hold of that hand of Christ and is drawn nearer and nearer to Himself. That is, I think, the best method of promoting spiritual life."

This steady stream of Christian spirituality through vocation flows down through the ages, and it alone is sufficient to the soul and to the world of humanity today. We have only to step into it, to set ourselves to learn it, and we will see its radiant power at work on the "job" where we are. If one

---

[2] Philips Brooks, *Best Methods of Promoting Spiritual Life*, (New York: Thomas Whittaker 2&3 Bible House), 12-13, 35.

will simply learn from Jesus how to do our work we will find the promise, "I am with you always," to be the sure basis of abundance of life, whatever the "job."

How God is in Business

By Dallas Willard (2001)[3]

My objective is to change people's minds. <u>I gave up a long time ago trying to get people to do things, and decided instead to help them think things through and come to a different view of matters.</u> My main goal is to help them come to a correct understanding of who they are and where they are, and then they, together with the Lord, can begin to participate in the right kinds of activities.

With this in mind, I want to address the topic, "How God is in Business." I'm going to use the term *business* rather generously. It will cover everyone who is here, and fundamentally the broader context of professional life that most of us exist in. But I want to speak in such a way that it covers all of us and the things we're doing to make a living, and beyond that, to serve our community.

Let me start with a passage from the apostle Paul, that great teacher and leader for Christ: "Slaves, in all things obey those who are your masters" (Colossians

[3] First published as Appendix A in Bill Heatley, *The Gift of Work*, NavPress, 2008.

3:22, NASB). Many people today will say, "Well, that's me!" But these were real slaves, and it certainly applies to all of us today who try to serve others by working. Paul goes on to say that slaves should obey their masters "not with external service,…but with sincerity of heart, fearing the Lord. Whatever you do, do your work heartily, as for the Lord rather than for men, knowing that from the Lord you will receive the reward of the inheritance" (verses 22-24, NASB). Note the simple starkness of the last sentence: "It is the Lord Christ whom you serve" (verse 24, NASB).

This is a radical change in the understanding of what work is, what a job is, and what business is, and it can only be understood in the context of the kingdom of God. I'm not going to try to exhort you to get God into business; I'm just going to try to explain to you two main ways that He *is* in business, and we have to come to terms with this, because He is there.

The first way is simply this: Business is God's arrangement. Human beings didn't think it up. They put some variations on it, but it is a part of God's design, by which human beings love and serve one another. It is an extension of the basic human relationships that we have in family, which reach out to neighbors and communities, and it is a fundamental structure of love in the kingdom of God. I'll say that again: **Business is a fundamental structure of love in the kingdom of God**.

That's where we have to start. We read in the Psalms and other Scriptures about how God looks down from Heaven and observes the hearts of human beings. I especially like 2 Chronicles, 16:9: "The eyes of the Lord move to and fro throughout the whole earth that He may strongly support those whose heart is completely His" NASB). That's a basic picture that we must never forget. God is on the job, business is His business, humanity is not a human project. Humanity is God's project, and He is bringing out of it an amazing community of redeemed souls, which He will dwell in for eternity. We each get to be a part of that.

One of the things I often point out in teaching about the kingdom of God is that our role in our present life is *training for reigning.* That applies to business. Often, when we look at business and the fine details, especially the religious business, it doesn't look like God is in control. That's because He has made space for us to learn to live under Him and to love our neighbor as ourselves, while we are at the same time loving Him with all our heart, soul, mind and strength. As a result, there's much professional tension today, in all of the professions. The old professions are of course the clergy, law and medicine. My work provides me with opportunities to talk to a lot of doctors' and lawyers' groups. It's unfortunate, but I think I can make a general statement today that nearly all in those professions feel like the conditions under which they practice their work militate against the very purpose for which they went into their work in the first place.

I meet a lot of ministers that testify to that same sort of thing. They're just beaten to death by the things that are pushed upon them in their job. I meet a lot of mothers who feel that way about it too. We move in a world that, it seems, constantly harasses us and distracts us from the purposes that in our heart of hearts we feel we should be fulfilling.

"The ABCs of Success"

We need to talk for a moment about why that is. It really is because the standards of success that are accepted and that people are held to in the various lines of work confuse us about what we're supposed to be doing. It's often said in church-growth circles that the ABCs of success in the church are "attendance," "buildings," and "cash." We understand where that's coming from because we can easily draw that conclusion by just standing on the sidelines and watching who gets applauded and rewarded.

Some time back it struck me that, when I was young, we didn't ask if our ministers were successful. Just to check my memory, I asked my wife, Jane, "Did we think of ministers in terms of success or not?" She confirmed to me that we really didn't think in those terms. We believed that they had a call in their lives and they were doing the best they could to fulfill that call. And we knew that sometimes they failed, and that some were more entertaining to listen to. Of course, there were many ministers who were not good speakers and others who were not well educated, yet they were faithful men who, over the years, did a tremendous work for God. But if you try to judge them by the ABCs, they flunk.

I watch my students go off to law school, all full of ideas. They're going to serve justice, and their hearts are aflame with it. They come back in two years pretty well squashed. And then, perhaps two years after that, I see them, and they have come to understand that the system of law they're involved in does not have an awful lot to do with justice.

I spoke to a group of doctors from Hollywood Presbyterian Hospital some years back, and nearly every one of them was arranging to retire. They were searching

12

to find a way to get out of the business and save themselves physically and financially. This is a tough thing. On the one hand it makes us want to ask, "So how *is* God in business?" Well, God is in business because He's in everything, and business is His arrangement. We need to respect that and know that. But on the other hand, when we look at the fine structure, we see there's a real problem. We need to spend some time talking about why that is so.

Love and Serve Others?

We live in a period of great moral confusion. When we think about serving others, for example, we need to ask, "What does that mean?" When we think about loving others, loving our neighbor, what does that mean? In Western culture today, there are two broad responses to love or service. Hardly anyone rejects love or service outright; they're seen as good things. And in business people emphasize the importance of service, but what does it mean?

Today when we talk about loving someone, it often means that we must be prepared to approve of what they desire, and the decisions that they make, and to help them fulfill those goals. So in effect we are told, "If you love me, you will do what I want you to do." Now that gives a whole new meaning to service. And that can even lead us, in the church situation, toward simply trying to do what people want in order to get them to come back.

The same principle is true at a business or in an educational institution. At the University of Southern California, where I teach, we have no meaningful undergraduate requirement in mathematics for the whole degree program. I venture that's true in more universities

13

than you might suppose. And the reason is because the students don't want it. That raises an issue: perhaps there's another meaning to love and service that we need to think about.

Here's a second meaning: To love and serve people means to favor what is good for them, and to be prepared to help them fulfill it, even if that means disapproving of their desires and decisions, and attempting to, as appropriate, prevent their fulfillment. The fact that someone wants something doesn't necessarily mean that it's in his best interest, does it?

Let me go over these two meanings again, because this is fundamental to the whole idea of serving others. One way of thinking about service is, "I love you, and I'll serve you by doing what you *want* me to do." That's perhaps one of the most common ideas today. The other idea is, "I love you, and I will serve you by doing what is *good* for you, whether you want it or not." You see the difference? Now, you might say to a young person, "You need to know mathematics whether you want it or not." It's a little late when they get to the university to do that, but that's another story.

Still, the difference here is what is good for you versus what you want. The issue is whether or not you can think in terms of serving people just by giving them what they want. And the answer is: You can't. You cannot do that. And in order to stand on this principle, you need a point of reference beyond what people want. That's where God comes back into business.

Meeting Needs

God gives us a point of reference for determining what is good for people independently of what they want.

14

That's why it's so important in the family to have this point of reference, but it's equally important in the schools, and it's equally important in business. If you look at it historically, if you look at the literature regarding business, you will see that _the aim of business is to make provision for the needs of the people in an area._ That's the aim of business. In older days it was largely physical needs, but today of course, in the age of information, it's going to involve intellectual or mechanical or technical needs—all kinds of needs to be met. Still, the basic aim of business is to make provision for the needs of the people in an area served.

Notice the way this is developing. If a business actually does make that provision, it is successful. Well, immediately the response comes back, "But does it make a lot of money?" Here I'm going to say something that will strike many people as heretical: The aim of business is not to make money. Just like the aim of churches is not to attract people. Is it important to make money? Yes it is. Is it important to attract people to church? Yes it is. But that's not the mark of success. And that's where we have to have a different place to stand.

I say to you very simply that the only place we can stand is in the teachings of Jesus Christ. He is the only one who can give us the guidance we need in order to serve others, whatever our line of work may be, and wherever we are in that line of work. We have to be able to stand there.

The Place of Discipleship

This brings us to the subject of discipleship. I want to apply it particularly to the area of work. _The place of discipleship is wherever I am now. It's wherever I am now, and_ _whatever I am doing now_. If we don't understand that, then most of our life will be left out of the place of discipleship. It may be home, it may be work, play, or church, but discipleship should take place wherever I am now.

When I go to work at USC and I walk into a class, that's my place of discipleship. That's the place where I am learning from Jesus how to do everything I do in the kingdom of God. I am constantly learning it, and I am a long way from the end of the lesson. Sometimes I'd prefer that the lessons would stop, but they don't, because life moves on and students are different and colleagues change. The challenges in the areas of thought that I write about and work in change, so I have to be reconciled to the fact that I am going to be a disciple of Jesus in my workplace from here on.

That's why it's important for me to understand that Jesus is, in fact, the smartest man in my field. He's the smartest man in your field. It doesn't matter what you're doing. If you're running a bank, or a mercantile company, or a manufacturing plant, or a government office, or whatever it is, He's the smartest man on that job.

So we're constantly in school under Jesus' authority and tutelage. He is our master and teacher. That's the teaching that Paul gives us again in Colossians: "Whatsoever you do, whether in word or deed, do it all in the name [that is on behalf of and in the power] of the Lord Jesus, giving thanks to God the Father through him" (3:17).

I'm not just giving a religious lesson—I'm talking about life. I'm saying that if we are going to accept God in business, we need to be the kind of people who can be godly in business. I remember Al McDonald, the head of

Jimmy Carter's White House staff, once came to a seminar I gave. After my presentation, he came up to me and asked, "How do you get Christianity into the boardroom?" My answer was very simple: "Have a Christian walk in and sit down." There isn't any other way.

Business is God's Business

That's the other part of the answer to the question, "How is God in business?" He is in business because the business is His, because the world is His. Not only the cattle but the Cadillac's on a thousand hills belong to Him, and the BMW's, too.[4] It all belongs to Him. But He has left a space where we have to make the choice to be His people in the midst of His world. And we have to overcome these dreadful moral confusions that rest upon our world. They prevent us from understanding that serving really involves giving people what is good for them, not merely pursuing their approval and granting their desires. I hope you see the difference between these, because this is the breakpoint upon which our culture is standing at present.[5]

---

[4] Psalm 50:10, "For every wild animal of the forest is mine, the cattle on a thousand hills."

[5] From Socrates and the ancient Greeks to our founding fathers, the possession of moral knowledge was considered utterly crucial for the survival of individuals and societies. "The life of the nation is secure only while the nation is honest, truthful, and virtuous." — Frederick Douglas. We have lost our way in this area and we are at risk. Calvin Coolidge wrote, "The foundations of our society and our government rest so much on the teachings of the Bible that it would be difficult to support them if faith in these teachings would cease to be practically universal in our country." We are close to

What is it to be a good person in business? We have a lot of courses now in business ethics and professional ethics that are not about ethics at all. Courses in professional ethics and texts in professional ethics are basically studies in how to stay out of trouble—*and that's not a high moral ideal.* The emphasis is on how to stay out of trouble with your clients, with your fellow professionals, and with the law. If you read those texts and go to conferences on these subjects, you'll see that they don't touch the basic issue in professional ethics, which is how to be a good person through your field of activity. Understanding how to be a good person—that's where the light has gone out in our culture. It comes as a real shock to many young people to realize that you could be successful and not be a good person. That's because they now are given no way of thinking about what it is to be a good person.

A morally good person is someone intent upon advancing the various goods of human life with which they are in effective contact. This individual does this in a manner that respects relative degrees of importance and the extent to which the actions of the person in question can actually promote the existence and maintenance of those goods—the various goods of human life. Being a good person yourself is among the most important of those goods. So to promote moral goodness in yourself and others is a very important part of being a good person. Elton Trueblood somewhere echoes the voice of older moralists that the only really good thing is a good person.

Our confusions now are so deep on these matters that most people cannot say exactly what it means to be

that point, and we have nothing capable of supporting those foundations should we reach it.

a good person and then put that idea into the context of their work. Young people especially have trouble here. I find older people have had enough experience to know they've got to do something about being good, and they usually have worked their way through to some sensible version of it. Of course, Christian folks normally feel like there's a great obligation on their part to bring Christ into work and make Him a substantial part of who they are as a teacher, a banker, a lawyer and so forth.

Sometimes the hardest people, I find, to get to believe they could be a disciple of Jesus in their work are lawyers and investment bankers. That's right where we need it the most – people who would be responsible in these areas, or in the area of education.

Love is the Center of Goodness

Who is a good person? From the Christian point of view, a good person is one who loves God with all his heart, soul, mind and strength, and loves his neighbor as himself (see Luke 10:27). And then we need to add that among Christians the ideal is a little higher. That is, we should love one another *as* Christ has loved us.

So love is the center of goodness. It's the driving force in all our activities. When I walk into my classes, if I don't love those students, I have failed. But suppose they believe I only love them if I give them what they want. Doing so would be to betray them, wouldn't it? So I must have an understanding of goodness that allows me to get beyond their wants and desires. I must stand as a whole and strong person who carries through with a consistent line of activity that will really help them, because if I only do what they want, it will ultimately harm them.

To accomplish this, I must take care of myself. I cannot just let myself go—I must train myself as a disciple of Jesus Christ. I have to learn how to be a whole person. I have to make sure that I don't make the mistake of thinking that I can, for example, just work hard and be successful. I reiterate this point because it's one of the major problems of our day: People believe that if they work hard enough, they'll become successful, and that's the chief aim in life.

A couple of weeks ago, I heard a man teach at the University of Beijing, and he talked about what has happened to young people in China and how they define success. It is simply money, money and more money. They go to the universities, and their object is to do the best they can in their courses, get the best possible positions, so they can make the most possible money. And that is as far as they go. We've got a lot of people in the U.S., too, many times in our churches, who really don't view success as anything beyond that. They do not understand what it means to be a whole person, living under God, with other people who are going through life on their way to eternity. That is a lost concept to them.

So as a disciple of Jesus, I have to know what kinds of things will help me be His kind of person, where I am. A significant part of this means I'm a student of His. I study Him, I study what He says, but I have to go beyond that and learn the practices that will enable me to stay steady in His word, and in His life, and in my work. Because discipleship is not just a matter of learning what He says, but learning to do everything I do in the way that He would do it if He were I.

So I have to have a pattern of discipline in my life that enables me to steadily feed and nourish my soul and my body with the things that will enable me to be God's person where I am. I'm not talking about being the local Christian nag. I'm talking about being the kind of person in whom God shines so brightly that people wonder what's going on. You remember Jesus' words, "Let your light so shine before men, that they will see your good works and glorify your Father who is in heaven" (Matthew 5:16 NASB).

You want a kind of light and power living in you that is so great that people never make the mistake of thinking it comes from you. Jesus said that, "a city set on a hill cannot be hidden" (Matthew 5:14, NASB). We don't have to nag. We don't have to be sure that we get in our negative points. Very often it's sufficient to stand up for righteousness by simply remaining in cheerful non-compliance with evil. Simply don't participate. When we're expected to lie, we don't lie. When we're expected to gossip, we don't gossip. When we're expected to hurt other people who have hurt us, we don't do that. You see, that's just a part of what comes from this light of Christ in us.

Your Hand In God's

We should also expect that there will be evidence of a supernatural hand of God in the work we do. That's a part of discipleship too. A part of discipleship is learning how to fulfill our responsibilities and complete our tasks in such a way that God will be manifestly present in that work.

So we have to have a range of disciplines that will help us stand and be steady. We have to be ready to practice the things that make us strong. William James once said, "Keep the faculty of effort alive in you by a little gratuitous exercise every day. That is, be systematically heroic in little unnecessary points." I like that language. He also said:

> Every day do something for no other reason than its difficulty, so that when the hour of dire need draws nigh, it may find you not unnerved and untrained to stand the test. Asceticism in this sort of thing is like the insurance which a man pays on his house and goods. The tax does him no good at the time, and possibly may never bring him a return, but if fire does come, his having paid it, it will be his salvation from ruin. So with the man who has daily inured himself to habits of concentrated attention, energetic volition, and self-denial in unnecessary things. He will stand like a tower when everything rocks around him, and his softer fellow mortals are winnowed like chaff in the blast."[6]

Now, that's a merely human approach. Add to it, "Take your cross and follow Christ." Now you step out of the merely human. You can't disregard the merely human, but you need to put on top of it the grace of God and discipleship to Christ that involves self-denial practiced in a regular way, both for the benefit of the quality of your work and the quality of your relationships; and as you do that, then you begin to see the fruit of a life that is lived fully in the kingdom of God.

---

[6] William James quoted in William Carl Rudiger *The Principles of Education* (New York: Houghton Mifflin, 1910), 275).

Aspects of Your Life

Take a look at this diagram. Think about your job, your ministry, your work and your life. (Everyone has a ministry. You don't have to be in full-time Christian work to have a ministry. We'll talk about that in just a moment.) It is extremely important for you to distinguish those things if you're going to take care of yourself and be the kind of person who can stand in the world of business as a whole person for Christ.

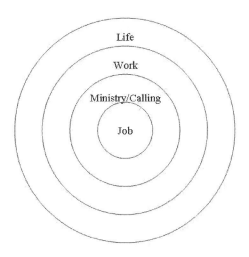

Let me just briefly describe them. Your **job** is what you get paid to do. If you don't have a job at this point in your life, that's all right. I have a lot of students who don't want a job, they want a position. A position is where you get paid whether you do anything or not! So your job is what you get paid to do. You can immediately see that for many people there's a problem in that their job will become their whole life. That's a threat that hangs over us.

Then there's your **ministry**, which is that part of God's work He has entrusted to you. There are some things that God specifically wants done in your time and in your place, and He's given those things to you to do. It may be a lot of different things. If our task is as pastor or teacher or something of that sort, then ministry may be a bigger part of our life. But even so, our job and our ministry are two different things.

Your work is the total amount of good that you will accomplish in your lifetime. For many of us, our family will be a large part of that. I say that because in being Christ's person in the world today, we need to make sure that we don't sacrifice our family to our ministry or to our job.

Encompassing all of this is your **life**. That's you. God is more interested in your life than he is in any of the other things there. He's more interested in the person you are becoming than in your work or your ministry or your job. If you are careful to distinguish between *who you are* and *what you do*, then you'll have a basis to stand in the face of the pressures that can tear you apart in this world. And you will be a whole person, and your family will be whole, and you'll do wonderful work, and you will bring God into your work wherever you may be, because you've allowed God to live in you completely. Now, if you don't, God will still bless you in some measure. You'll still go to Heaven when you die, if you trust Jesus, but your life may be rather sad.

Cultivating the Garden of Your Life

What follows is a touching poem that helps us see the pathos of a life in which we have not received God fully.

The wind, one brilliant day, called to my soul,
    with an odor of jasmine —

"In return for the odor of my jasmine
    I'd like all the odor of your roses."

 "I have no roses;
    all the flowers in my garden are dead."

"Well then, I'll take the withered petals
    and the yellow leaves
    and the waters of the fountain."

The wind left. And I wept.
    And I said to myself:

"What have you done with the garden
    that was entrusted to you?"[7]

To each of us is given a garden. It is our life. God gives us all the grace and wisdom we will need if we will cultivate it under Him. And when we do, wherever we are in life, God will be there.

---

[7] Antonio Machado, "The Wind One Brilliant Day," in trans. Robert Bly, *The Winged Energy of Delight* (New York: HarperCollins, 2004) 69.

The Business of Business

By Dallas Willard (2006)[8]

What is business (manufacturing, commerce) for? Today the spontaneous response to this question is: The business of business is to make money for those who are engaged in it. In fact, this answer is now regarded as so obvious that you might be thought stupid or uninformed if you even ask the question. But that is only one of the effects of the pervasive miseducation that goes on in contemporary society, which fosters an understanding of success essentially in terms of fame, position and material goods. However, that only reflects a quite recent view of the professions—of which we will here assume business to be one—and, even today, is definitely *not* the view of success in professional life shared by the public in general. No business or other profession that advertises its 'services' announces to the public that it is there for the purpose of enriching itself or those involved in it. With one accord they all say their purpose is service, not

---

[8] First published in The Trinity Forum's online journal, October 2006. The Trinity Forum is a nonprofit organization that works to cultivate networks of leaders whose integrity and vision will renew culture and promote human freedom and flourishing. Learn more at www.ttf.org.

serve-us. I have never met "professionals" who would tell their clients that they were there just for their own self-interest. Still, many professionals today are dominated by self-interest, and that is the source of the constant stream of moral failures that occupies our courts and what we now call "news." And many who would never say it publicly really do think of their success in terms of self-advancement, and will say so "after hours." The role of the "professional" is really a moral role in society, and not just one of technical expertise in the marketplace of untrammeled competition.

The older tradition of the profession as, at bottom, *a moral role in society* was more obvious and defensible before the days of mass society and urban anonymity in which the individual doctor, lawyer, etc. more or less disappears as a person living together with other persons. The special training, position and respect given them was, in other days, an appropriate response to the special and potentially self-sacrificing good that they made available to ordinary people in the social setting: to the public or 'common' good, as used to be said. With respect to the merchant or manufacturer there has always been less clarity about this than with the older professions of clergy, medicine and law, but his or her special position and power in the community was nonetheless understood to bring with them unique and unavoidable moral responsibilities.

Writing of this in 1860, John Ruskin remarks: "The fact is that people never have had clearly explained to them the true functions of a merchant with respect to other people. He then puts what we today would call "business" in the context of the "Five great intellectual professions" necessary to the life of "every civilized nation." With respect to that nation:

> "The Soldier's profession is to *defend* it.
> The Pastor's to *teach* it.
> The Physician's, to *keep it in health*.
> The Lawyer's to *enforce justice* in it
> The Merchant's to *provide* for it. "[9]

He appends to this list: "And the duty of all these men is, on due occasion, to *die* for it." The soldier to die "rather than leave his post in battle," the physician "rather than leave his post in plague," the pastor "rather than teach falsehood," the lawyer "rather than countenance injustice," and the merchant...rather than...*what?* It is here, Ruskin acknowledges, that people are apt to be unable to finish the thought. What is it that the "merchant" would die rather than do?

The answer to this question is supplied by the merchant's or manufacturer's function and the good that it supplies to the people in his community. His task is to *provide for* the community. His function is not to pluck from the community the means of his own self-aggrandizement. "It is no more his function," Ruskin continues, "to get profit for himself out of that provision than it is a clergyman's function to get his stipend. The stipend is a due and necessary adjunct, but not the object of his life, if he be a true clergyman, any more than his fee (or *honorarium*) is the object of life to a true physician. Neither is his fee the object of life to a true merchant. All three, if true men, have a work to be done irrespective of

---

[9] All quotations are from "Lecture I" of Ruskin's book *Unto This Last*. Many editions. This lecture is titled, "The Roots of Honor." See the longer excerpt in Appendix A.

fee.... That is to say, he has to understand to their very root the qualities of the thing he deals in, and the means of obtaining or producing it; and he has to apply all his sagacity and energy to the producing or obtaining it in perfect state, and distributing it at the cheapest possible price where it is most needed."

Ruskin proceeds to emphasize the responsibility of the "merchant" for the well-being of those in his employ. The merchant has a direct governance over those who work for him. So "...it becomes his duty, not only to be always considering how to produce what he sells in the purest and cheapest forms, but how to make the various employments involved in the production or transference of it most beneficial to the men employed." Hence the function of business requires "...the highest intelligence, as well as patience, kindness, and tact, ... all his energy ... and to give up, if need be, his life in such way as it may be demanded of him." As the captain of a ship is duty-bound to be the last to leave the ship in disaster, "...so the manufacturer, in any commercial crisis or distress, is bound to take the suffering of it with his men, and even to take more of it for himself than he allows his men to feel; as a father would in a famine, shipwreck, or battle, sacrifice himself for his son."

That Ruskin may not be left to stand alone in the field, we also cite the words of Louis Brandeis, one of the greatest of past American leaders of thought and government. In his Commencement Day address to Brown University of October 1912, titled "Business—A Profession,"[10] Brandeis remarks that:

---

[10] First published in *Business—A Profession,* (Boston: Small, Maynard & Co., Publishers, 1914). See the longer excerpt in Appendix B.

The recognized professions…definitely reject the size of financial return as the measure of success. They select as their test, excellence of performance in the broadest sense—and include, among other things, advance in particular occupation and service to the community. These are the basis of all worthy reputations in the recognized professions. In them a large income is the ordinary incident of success; but he who exaggerates the value of the incident is apt to fail of real success. … In the field of modern business, so rich in opportunity for the exercise of man's finest and most varied mental faculties and moral qualities, mere money-making cannot be regarded as the legitimate end.

Brandeis gives most of his lecture to illustrating "real success" in business, "comparable with the scientist's, the inventor's, the statesman's," from the careers of contemporary businessmen around the turn of the last century. He, like Ruskin, emphasizes the *nobility* of the "merchant's" function. If we take such careers as models, he says, "Then the term 'Big business' will lose its sinister meaning, and will take on a new significance. Big business will then mean business big not in bulk or power, but great in service and grand in manner."

Well, needless to say, this change of meaning has not yet happened. Texts by Ruskin and by Brandeis, along with similar ones,[11] are not popular references in our

---

[11] The "Progressive Movement" of the latter 19th Century and the first part of the 20th Century was, in large part, an effort to implement in the political and social life of America the kind of idealism, somewhat toned down to be sure, expressed by Ruskin, T. H. Green and Brandeis. What happened to that movement—

schools of business today. These schools, for all their good, are, instead, far too much given to "The excuses which selfishness makes for itself in the mouths of cultivated men,"[12] to quote another person from the times of Ruskin and Brandeis. Certainly in business one must make a profit, and one's business must survive if it is to serve. But not at the expense of the public good and the well-being of individuals who depend on you—not, for example, if you must sell tainted food or shoddily furniture or electronic devices to stay afloat or thrive. And certainly not as *the* aim or goal of those involved in business. It is not enough to say that "the market" will drive you out if you don't do what is right.

That slogan, with its grain of truth, is brain surgery with a meat cleaver, at best; and in fact it rarely turns out to be true. It serves at all only because, at this particular time in our history, the weight of *moral calling* and *moral character* is unable to serve as established points of reference for individual practice and public policy. They are not treated as aspects of *reality* which must be appealed to in judgment and with which any decent person must come to terms. There is no legitimating support, therefore, for the idealism of young people who go into the professions or the justifiable demands of the public to be served. It is a ***convincing framework of***

---

how it went sour through the course of events, and was gutted of its genius by currents of thoughts without viable moral content— would be a highly instructive study for any person devoted to understanding our current social and personal situation in America. A good place to start might be *Who Were the Progressives?*, Glenda Gilmore, editor, Boston: St. Martin's Press, 2002), and Michael McGerr, *A Fierce Discontent: The Rise and Fall of the Progressive Movement in America, 1870-1920*, (New York: Oxford University Press, 2003).

[12] The words of T. H. Green in §208 of his *Prolegomena to Ethics*.

calling and character that must be restored if professional life is to be directed in a manner which— surely everyone deep-down knows—is suited to its function as provider and protector of the public good and of individuals throughout our neighborhoods and beyond. The greatest challenge to an officially Post-Christian world is to provide that framework. To this point it is not doing very well with the task.[13] Surely the best course—find a better who may—is to take up one's profession as an appointment from God, through intelligent discipleship to Jesus Christ. This provides a time tested and experiential foundation and framework for professional life that yields the nobility seen by Ruskin and Brandeis—and much more.

---

[13] But see, by contrast, Os Guinness's indispensable book, *The Call*, (Nashville: Word Publishing, 1998). See, as well, the many treatments of the spiritual life by Phillips Brooks (1835-1893).

Appendices

Whenever Willard taught about virtues, ethics, business, or the professions he would ensure his students received and read the two papers below. He wanted to provide them with a way of thinking about business that would focus their minds on the good and virtuous aspects of their chosen field of endeavor. They are in the Appendix in the excerpted form that he used when distributing them to his students.

Unto This Last

By John Ruskin (1907)[14]

The fact is, that people never have had clearly explained to them the true functions of a merchant with respect to other people. I should like the reader to be very clear about this.

Five great intellectual professions, relating to daily necessities of life, have hitherto existed—three exist necessarily, in every civilized nation:

> The Soldier's profession is to *defend* it.
> The Pastor's, to *teach* it.
> The Physician's, to *keep it in health*.

---

[14] John Ruskin was a profound thinker who influenced Dallas in his views regarding work, and culture. The book title, *Unto This Last*, comes from the Parable of the Workers in the Vineyard (Mt 20:1-16), when the vineyard owner pays all the workers equally at the end of the day and states, "I will give unto this last, even as unto thee" (KJV). Ruskin turns the phrase into a lens for us to view our devotion to our profession and the service it provides to the public. The book began as a series of four articles published in *Cornhill Magazine* in 1860. He intended to publish seven articles, but each successive article became more controversial, so the magazine refused to continue publishing the articles. This excerpt is from chapter one (entitled" The Roots of Honour").

The Lawyer's, to *enforce justice* in it.
The Merchant's, to *provide* for it.

And the duty of all these men is, on due occasion, to *die* for it.

"*On due occasion*," namely:

The Soldier, rather than leave his post in battle.
The Physician, rather than leave his post in plague.
The Pastor, rather than teach Falsehood.
The Lawyer, rather than countenance Injustice.
The Merchant—What is *his* "due occasion" of death?

It is the main question for the merchant, as for all of us. For, truly, the man who does not know when to die, does not know how to live.

The Duty of the Merchant

Observe, the merchant's function (or manufacturer's, for in the broad sense in which it is here used the word must be understood to include both) is to provide for the nation. It is no more his function to get profit for himself out of that provision than it is a clergyman's function to get his stipend. The stipend is a due and necessary adjunct, but not the object, of his life, if he be a true clergyman, any more than his fee (or *honorarium*) is the object of life to a true physician. Neither is his fee the object of life to a true merchant. All three, if true men, have a work to be done irrespective of fee—to be done even at any cost, or for quite the contrary of fee; the pastor's function being to teach, the physician's to heal, and the merchant's, as I have said, to provide. That is to say, he has to understand to the very root the qualities of the thing he deals in, and the means of obtaining or producing it; and he has to apply all his sagacity and energy to the producing or obtaining it in perfect state, and distributing it at the cheapest possible price where it is most needed.

And because the production or obtaining of any commodity involves necessarily the agency of many lives and hands, the merchant becomes in the course of his business the master and governor of large masses of men in a more direct, though less confessed way, than a military officer or pastor; so that on him falls, in great part, the responsibility for the kind of life they lead: and it becomes his duty, not only to be always considering how to produce what he sells in the purest and cheapest forms, but how to make the various employments involved in the production, or transference of it, most beneficial to the men employed.

And as into these two functions, requiring for their right exercise the highest intelligence, as well as patience, kindness, and tact, the merchant is bound, as soldier or physician is bound, to give up, if need be, his life, in such way as it may be demanded of him. Two main points he has in his providing function to maintain: first, his engagements (faithfulness to engagements being the real root of all possibilities in commerce); and, secondly, the perfectness and purity of the thing provided; so that, rather than fail in any engagement, or consent to any deterioration, adulteration, or unjust and exorbitant price of that which he provides, he is bound to meet fearlessly any form of distress, poverty, or labor, which may, through maintenance of these points, come upon him.

Again: in his office as governor of the men employed by him, the merchant or manufacturer is invested with a distinctly paternal authority and responsibility. In most cases, a youth entering a commercial establishment is withdrawn altogether from home influence; his master must become his father, else he has, for practical and constant help, no father at hand: in all cases the master's authority together with the general tone and atmosphere of his business, and the character of the men with whom the youth is compelled in the course of it to associate, have more immediate and pressing weight than the home influence, and will usually neutralize it either for good or evil, so that the only means which the master has of doing justice to the men employed by him is to ask himself sternly whether he is dealing with such subordinate as he would with his own son, if compelled by circumstances to take such a position.

Supposing the captain of a frigate saw it right, or were by any chance obliged, to place his own son in the position of a common sailor; as he would then treat his son, he is bound always to treat every one of the men under him. So, also, supposing the master a manufactory saw it right, or were by any chance obliged, to place his own son in the position of an ordinary workman; as he would then treat his son, he is bound always to treat every one of his men. This is the only effective, true, or practical RULE which can be given on this point of political economy.

And as the captain of a ship is bound to be the last man to leave his ship in case of wreck, and to share his last crust with sailors in case of famine, so the manufacturer, in any commercial crisis or distress, is bound to take the suffering of it with his men, and even to take more of it for himself than he allows his men to feel; as a father would in a famine, shipwreck, or battle, sacrifice himself for his son.

All which sounds very strange: the only real strangeness in the matter being, nevertheless, that it should so sound. For all this is true, and that not partially nor theoretically, but everlastingly and practically: all other doctrine than this respecting matters political being false in premises, absurd in deduction, and impossible in practice, consistently with any progressive state of national life; all the life which we now possess as a nation showing itself in the resolute denial and scorn, by a few strong minds and faithful hearts, of the economic principles taught to our multitudes, which principles, so far as accepted, lead straight to national destruction. Respecting the modes and forms of destruction to which they lead, and, on the other hand, respecting the farther practical working of true polity, I hope to reason further in a following paper.

Business: A Profession

By Louis D. Brandeis (1914)[15]

Each commencement season we are told by the college reports the number of graduates who have selected the professions as their occupations and the number of those who will enter business. The time has come for abandoning such a classification. Business should be, and to some extent already is, one of the professions. The once meagre list of the learned professions is being constantly enlarged. Engineering in its many branches already takes rank beside law, medicine and theology. Forestry and scientific agriculture are securing places of

---

[15] This commencement address, delivered at Brown University 1912, was first published in *System*, October 1912. It was then published in 1914 as chapter 1 of Brandeis' second book, *Business—A Profession*, a collection of speeches and magazine articles written before his confirmation to the Supreme Court. This essay promotes the idea of business as a recognized profession, on a par with law or medicine, due to its valuable contributions and obligations to society. The text of the book is available in its entirety on the website of the Louis D. Brandeis School of Law Library.

honor. The new professions of manufacturing, of merchandising, of transportation and of finance must soon gain recognition. The establishment of business schools in our universities is a manifestation of the modern conception of business.

The peculiar characteristics of a profession as distinguished from other occupations, I take to be these:

First. A profession is an occupation for which the necessary preliminary training is intellectual in character, involving knowledge and to some extent learning, as distinguished from mere skill.

Second. It is an occupation which is pursued largely for others and not merely for one's self.

Third. It is an occupation in which the amount of financial return is not the accepted measure of success.

Is not each of these characteristics found today in business worthily pursued?

The field of knowledge requisite to the more successful conduct of business has been greatly widened by the application to industry not only of chemical, mechanical and electrical science, but also the new science of management; by the increasing difficulties involved in adjusting the relations to labor to capital; by the necessary intertwining of social with industrial problems; by the ever extending scope of state and federal regulation of business. Indeed, mere size and territorial expansion have compelled the business man to enter upon new and broader fields of knowledge in order to match his achievements with his opportunities.

This new development is tending to make business an applied science. Through this development the relative value in business of the trading instinct and of mere shrewdness have, as compared with other faculties, largely diminished. The conception of trade itself has changed. The old idea of a good bargain was a transaction in which one man got the better of another. The new idea of a good contract is a transaction which is good for both parties to it.

Under these new conditions, success in business must mean something very different from mere money-making. In business the able man ordinarily earns a larger income than one less able. So does the able man in the recognized professions in law, medicine or engineering; and even in those professions more remote from money-making, like the ministry, teaching or social work. The world's demand for efficiency is so great and the supply so small, that the price of efficiency is high in every field of human activity.

The recognized professions, however, definitely reject the size of the financial return as the measure of success. They select as their test, excellence of performance in the broadest sense—and include, among other things, advance in the particular occupation and service to the community. These are the basis of all worthy reputation in the recognized professions. In them a large income is the ordinary incident of success; but he who exaggerates the value of the incident is apt to fail of real business.

To the business of today a similar test must be applied. True, in business the earning of profit is something more than an incident of success. It is an essential condition of success; because the continued absence of profit itself spells failure. But while loss spells failure, large profits do not connote success. Success must be sought in business also in excellence of performance; and in business, excellence of performance manifests itself, among other things, in the advancing of methods and processes; in the improvement of products;

in more perfect organization, eliminating friction as well as waste; in bettering the condition of the workingmen, developing their faculties and promoting their happiness; and in the establishment of right relation with customers and with the community.

In the field of modern business, so rich in opportunity for the exercise of man's finest and most varied mental faculties and moral qualities, mere money-making cannot be regarded as the legitimate end. Neither can mere growth in bulk or power be admitted as a worthy ambition. Nor can a man nobly mindful of his serious responsibilities to society, view business as a game; since with the conduct of business human happiness or misery is inextricably interwoven.

Real success in business is to be found in achievements comparable rather with those of the artist or the scientist, of the inventor or the statesman. And the joys sought in the profession of business must be like their joys and not the mere vulgar satisfaction which is experienced in the acquisition of money, in the exercise of power or in the frivolous pleasure of mere winning.

It was such real success, comparable with the scientist's, the inventor's, the statesman's, which marked the career of William H. McElwain of Boston, who died in 1908 at the age of forty-one. He had been in business on his own account but thirteen years. Starting without means, he left a fortune, all of which had been earned in the competitive business of shoe manufacturing, without the aid of either patent or trademark. That shows McElwain did not lack the money-making faculty. His company's sales grew from $75,957 in 1895 to $8,691,274 in 1908. He became thus one of the largest shoe manufacturers in the world. That shows he did not lack either ambition or organizing ability. The working capital required for this rapidly growing business was obtained by him without surrendering to outside investors or to bankers any share in the profits of business: all the stock in his company being owned either by himself or his active associates. That shows he did not lack financial skill.

But this money-making faculty, organizing ability and financial skill were with him servants, not masters. He worked for nobler ends than mere accumulation or lust of power. In those thirteen years McElwain made so many advances in the methods and practices of the long-established and prosperous branch of industry in which he was engaged, that he may be said to have revolutionized shoe manufacturing. He found it a trade; he left it an applied science.

This is the kind of thing he did: in 1902 the irregularity in the employment of the shoe worker was brought to his attention. He came greatly impressed with its economic waste, with the misery to the worker and the demoralization which attended it. Irregularity of employment is the worst and most extended of industrial evils. Even in fairly prosperous times the workingmen of America are subjected to enforced idleness and loss of earnings, on the average, probably ten to twenty percent of their working time. The irregularity of employment was no greater in the McElwain factories than in the other shoe factories. The condition was not so bad in shoe manufacturing as in many other branches of industry. But it was bad enough; for shoe manufacturing was a seasonal industry. Most manufacturers closed their factories twice a year. Some manufacturers had two additional slack periods.

This irregularity had been accepted by the trade—by manufacturers and workingmen alike—as inevitable. It had been bowed to as if it were a law of nature—a cross to be borne with resignation. But with McElwain an evil recognized was a condition to be remedied; and he set his great mind to solving the problem of irregularity of employment in his own factories; just as Wilbur Wright applied his mind to the aeroplane, as Bell, his mind to the telephone, and as Edison, his mind to the problems of electric light. Within a few years irregularity of employment had ceased in the McElwain factories; and before his death every one of his many thousand employees could find work three hundred and five days in the year.

Closely allied with the establishment of regularity of employment was the advance made by McElwain in introducing punctual delivery of goods manufactured by his company. Shoes are manufactured mainly upon orders; and the orders are taken on samples submitted. The samples are made nearly a year before the goods are sold to the consumer. Samples for the shoes which will be bought in the spring and summer of 1913 were made in the early summer of 1912. The solicitation of orders on these samples began in the late summer. The manufacture of the shoes commences in November; and the order is filled before July.

Dates of delivery are fixed, of course, when orders are taken; but the dates fixed had not been taken very seriously by the manufacturers; and the trade was greatly annoyed by irregularities in delivery. McElwain recognized the business waste and inconvenience attendant upon such unfulfilled promises. He insisted that an agreement to deliver on a certain day was as binding as an agreement to pay a note on a certain day.

He knew that to make punctual delivery possible, careful study and changes in the methods of manufacture

48

and of distribution were necessary. He made the study; he introduced the radical changes found necessary; and he so perfected his organization that customers could rely absolutely upon delivery on the day fixed. Scientific management practically eliminated the recurring obstacles of the unexpected. To attain this result business invention of a high order was of course necessary—invention directed to the departments both of production and of distribution.

The career of the Filenes of Boston affords another example of success in professionalized business. In 1891 the Filenes occupied two tiny retail stores in Boston. The floor space of each was only twenty feet square. One was a glove stand, the other a women's specialty store. Twenty years later their sales were nearly $5,000,000 a year. In September, 1912, they moved into a new building with more than nine acres of floor space. But the significant thing about their success is not their growth in size or in profits. The trade offers many other examples of similar growth. The pre-eminence of the Filenes lies in the advance which has been made in the nature, the aims and ideals of retailing, due to their courage, initiative, persistence and fine spirit. They have applied minds of a high order and a fine ethical sense to the prosaic and seemingly uninterested business of selling women's garments. Instead of remaining petty tradesmen, they have become, in every sense of the word, great merchants.

The Filenes recognized that the function of retail distribution should be undertaken as a social service, equal in dignity and responsibility to the function of production; and that it should be studied with equal intensity in order that the service may be performed with high efficiency, with great economy and with nothing more than a fair profit to the retailer. They recognized that to serve their own customers properly, the relations of the retailer to the producer must be fairly and scientifically adjusted; and, among other things, that it was the concern of the retailer to know whether the goods which he sold were manufactured under conditions which were fair to the workers—fair as to wages, hours of work and sanitary conditions.

But the Filenes recognized particularly their obligations to their own employees. They found as the common and accepted conditions in large retail stores, that the employees had no voice as to the conditions or rules under which they were to work; that the employees had no appeal from policies prescribed by the management; and that in the main they were paid the lowest rate of wages possible under competitive conditions.

In order to insure a more just arrangement for those working in their establishment, the Filenes provided three devices:

First. A system of self-government for employees, administered by the store co-operative association. Working through this association, the employees have the right to appeal from and to veto policies laid down by the management. They may adjust the conditions under which employees are to work, and, in effect, prescribe conditions for themselves.

Second. A system of arbitration, through the operation of which individual employees can call for an adjustment of differences that may exist between themselves and the management as to the permanence of employment, wages, promotion or conditions of work.

Third. A minimum wage scale, which provides that no woman or girl shall work in their store at a wage less than eight dollars a week, no matter what her age may be or what grade of position she may fill.

The Filenes have thus accepted and applied the principles of industrial democracy and of social justice. But they have done more—they have demonstrated that the introduction of industrial democracy and of social justice is at least consistent with marked financial success. They assert that the greater efficiency of their employees shows industrial democracy and social justice to be money-makers. The so-called "practical business man," the narrow money-maker without either vision or ideals, who hurled against Filenes, as against McElwain, the silly charge of being "theorists," has been answered even on his own low plane of material success.

McElwain and the Filenes are of course exceptional men; but there are in America today many with like perception and like spirit. The paths broken by such pioneers will become the peopled highways. Their exceptional methods will become accepted methods. Then the term "Big business" will lose its sinister meaning, and will take on a new significance. "Big business" will then mean business big not in bulk or power, but great in service and grand in manner. "Big business" will mean professionalized business, as distinguished from the occupation of petty trafficking or mere money-making. And as the profession of business develops, the great industrial and social problems expressed in the present social unrest will one by one find solution.

About the Author

DALLAS WILLARD (1935–2013) was a highly esteemed leader of Christian thought, as well as a Professor of Philosophy at the University of Southern California. His writings focus on what it means to follow Christ today, with a robust challenge to some contemporary understandings of discipleship and refreshing insights into God's gracious calling on our lives. In all his work, Willard displays a scholarly acumen and a pastor's heart, seeking to integrate philosophy, theology, and ethics with practical discipleship and Christian day-to-day living.

Dr. Willard taught at USC from 1965 until his retirement in 2012, and was Director of the School of Philosophy from 1982-1985. He also held visiting appointments at UCLA (1969) and the University of Colorado (1984). He mentored many young graduate students who are now making an impact for Christ in their work as philosophy professors engaged in outstanding scholarship. His philosophical publications are mainly in the areas of epistemology, the philosophy of mind and of logic, and on the philosophy of Edmund Husserl, including extensive translations of Husserl's early writings from German into English.

Many consider Dr. Willard to be one of today's most brilliant Christian thinkers. Richard Foster, author of the book *Celebration of Discipline*, says of Dallas Willard, "Rarely have I found an author so penetrating in his intellect combined with so generous a spirit." Others believe his ability to engage the modern skeptic is reminiscent of C.S. Lewis. More of his writing and teaching may be found on his website: www.dwillard.org.

ALSO BY DALLAS WILLARD

The Divine Conspiracy:
Rediscovering Our Hidden Life in God

The Spirit of the Disciplines:
Understanding How God Changes Lives

Hearing God:
Developing a Conversational Relationship with God

Renovation of the Heart:
Putting on the Character of Christ

The Disappearance of Moral Knowledge
(with Steve Porter, Aaron Preston & Gregg Ten Elshof)

Knowing Christ Today:
Why We Can Trust Spiritual Knowledge

The Divine Conspiracy Continued:
Fulfilling God's Kingdom on Earth
(with Gary Black Jr.)

Living in Christ's Presence:
Final Words on Heaven and the Kingdom of God
(with John Ortberg)

The Allure of Gentleness:
Defending the Faith in the Manner of Jesus

Life Without Lack:
Living in the Fullness of Psalm 23

The Great Omission:
Reclaiming Jesus's Essential Teachings on Discipleship

Logic and the Objectivity of Knowledge:
A Study in Husserl's Philosophy

Dallas Willard Ministries equips people to live in a daily interactive relationship with God through a fresh hearing of Jesus' life and teachings.

DWMinistries@DWillard.org

www.DallasWillardMinistries.org

Made in the USA
Middletown, DE
02 November 2022